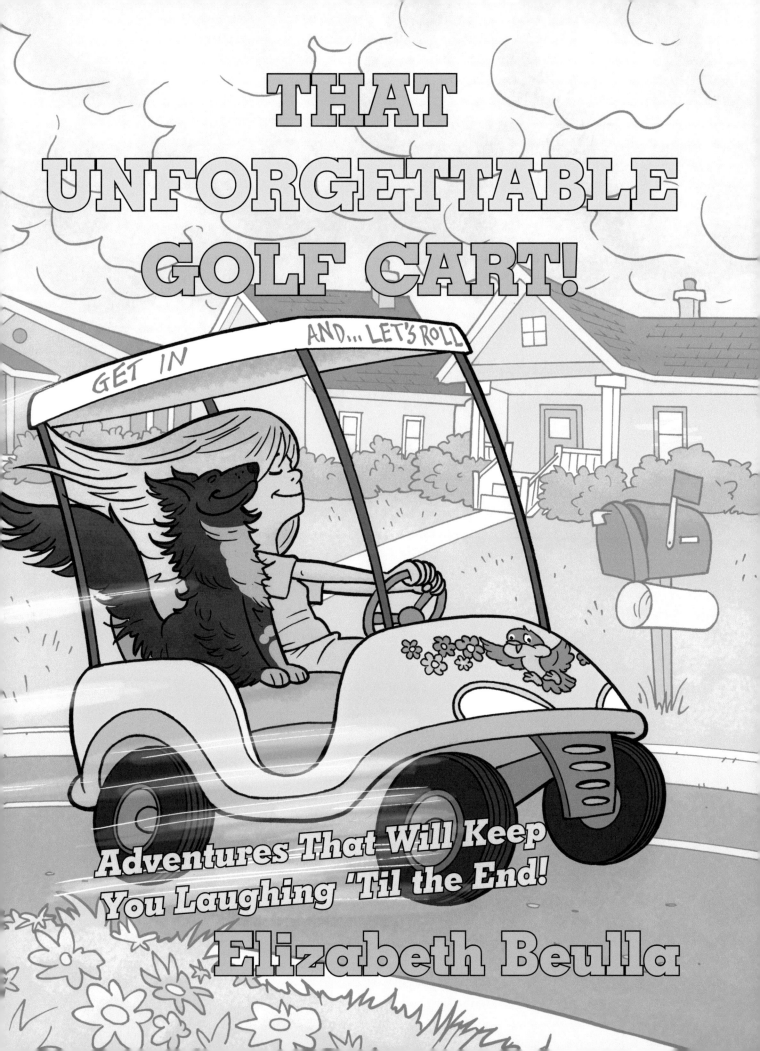

Archway Publishing books may be ordered through booksellers or by contacting:

Archway Publishing
1663 Liberty Drive
Bloomington, IN 47403
www.archwaypublishing.com
1 (888) 242-5904

ISBN: 978-1-4808-6684-3 (sc)
ISBN: 978-1-4808-6682-9 (hc)
ISBN: 978-1-4808-6683-6 (e)

Print information available on the last page.

Archway Publishing rev. date: 09/17/2018

*To my brave Mother who has always believed in me and encouraged me.*

# The Surviving Golf Cart

My dream of freedom is the wind blowing through my hair as I go out and about. It all started when I visited Aunt Sally, who lives in Florida, one February. When I entered her driveway, the sight of her golf cart made my eyes light up. I couldn't wait to try it. It was scary but challenging. I was very careful not to hit anything. It was so much fun that I didn't want to stop driving it. I drove that cart most of the time I was in Florida. Once home, I saved my money and did odd jobs around the house to earn money to buy my own golf cart.

A year later, I had enough to buy my golf cart, and the fun began in my neighborhood. One day I drove to my friend Alisha's house and missed her driveway. I hit the big oak tree standing in her front yard. Bang! I put the cart in reverse and saw there was a big chunk out the tree.

Luckily, I knew Alisha's mom would forgive me for running into her tree. The golf cart was not damaged, so I was very fortunate. The rest of the summer went by without incident, and my cart and I just had fun cruising around the neighborhood.

The following year, as soon as the weather was nice, my niece and I drove my golf cart from my house through the woods to a nearby ice cream place. We each had an ice cream, looked at flowers, and talked to friends. When we went to leave to go home, I tried to turn around the golf cart, but we went up on a curve and got stuck. One of the tires popped, and we were stranded at the ice cream store. I called my mom, who had been looking all over for my niece and I.

When I told her what happened, she lectured me big time about my driving skills, or lack of, and told me I was in trouble for making her worry. That was the big trouble event of that spring.

Summer was coming soon, and I was preparing for driver's education. Since I had some exciting experiences in my golf cart, I was hopeful it would be easier to learn how to drive an actual car.

I am glad I had a few years of driving experience with my golf cart before getting behind the wheel of a car. I know how teenagers drive and hope I drive better than most. I still like the wind in my hair, but I'll have to be happy with a convertible or something like that!

# Not Just an Ordinary Golf Cart

Golf carts are known for transporting golfers on golf courses, right? This wasn't the case for a thirteen-year-old. After a family trip, I set a goal to one day buy my own golf cart. Since no other young teen I knew had one, I was determined to be the first. After months of saving and help from my parents, I achieved my goal. I didn't want too many sunburns, so I had a roof put on it.

    The front of the cart looked too ordinary and blah, so I picked out decals at the store. Can you guess what I picked? A big Tweety Bird along with flowers to put on the sides of Tweety! Let me guess you're probably thinking thirteen years old is too old for someone to like Tweety Bird. That is probably true, but I thought I was ready to ride in style!

In the back of the cart was a back seat with a seat belt attached. The seat belt material was tied to each side of the handles on the cart. As people hopped on the seat, the material came together and buckled, just like on a school bus. The cart was uniquely decorated not only on the front but on the rear as well. At the top of the cart, on the edge of the roof, was a word decal that told the rules of the cart, so to speak. It read, "Get in. Hold on. And … Let's Roll!" The golf cart was known as the "Tweety Mobile."

# That Unforgettable Golf Cart

The wind that blew through my hair continues to blow. I have several stories to share about my golf cart that weren't even mentioned in the first story. Because it was an unforgettable time, why not continue sharing the adventures?

I was so excited to have a golf cart that I picked up a friend and gave her a ride. We rode around the neighborhood for so long that the golf cart's batteries went dead! We were left stranded on a sidewalk. *Now what?* I wondered. I knew we had to do something. I sat in the cart to steer while my friend pushed as hard as she could. Going uphill was the worst! After a long time, my friend and I finally reached my driveway. It was time to plug in the cart's charger and let the battery recharge for the next day.

Rise and shine! It was time to ride. As I grabbed the keys to the cart, I noticed my dog, Missy, was at my feet, wagging her tail. "Wanna go buh-bye?" "Woof! Woof!" I grabbed the leash, and out the door we went. Missy quickly jumped onto the cart and was ready to go, so off we went. My dog and I were off on an adventure. The wind not only blew through my hair but also Missy's fur.

When we returned home, Missy refused to get off the cart. "Come on, Missy." It was clear the dog liked that cart much more than going for a walk. From that point on, whenever I left in the golf cart, with or without friends, Missy went too.

The dog isn't the only unusual character in this story. One day while sitting in the kitchen, my sister and I heard the sound of the golf cart going backward. She ran out to the garage to find that her three-and-a-half-year-old son, Andrew, was flying down the road. As she chased him, shouting, "Stop that cart right now!" he was cracking up in laughter. Andrew kept going until he just missed hitting the stop sign.

My sister jumped in, took over the driving, and got the cart—and Andrew—back home. "Andrew, how did you start that golf cart?" she asked him.

"With this," he answered, picking up the end of a basketball needle pump. "I hotwired it!" We were shocked to hear these words from a three-year-old!

"Where in the world did you learn that?" she asked.

"The TV!" Then Andrew knew he was in trouble and started crying. "Mama, I sorry!"

The next day at school, the story of the latest golf cart drama quickly spread. As soon as class started, I heard from a boy in my class and my next-door neighbor who had witnessed the entire scene. He explained how he was standing in his front yard, and then all of a sudden, he saw this little boy zooming down the road, laughing hysterically. Then he noticed a woman running as fast as she could to catch him. "All I could do was cross my arms and shake my head," explained the neighbor kid.

The teacher looked at me and did her best not to laugh, asking if this was true. "Sounds crazy, doesn't it?" The good news was that no one got hurt!

# The Neighborhood Mailbox

One day while riding around, I decided to go to the neighborhood down the road to a friend's house. I gave him a ride in my golf cart. It was a beautiful day, not a cloud in the sky. My friend Alex shouted, "Hey, I want to touch my mailbox while driving by it." I approached the mailbox but came a little too close and hit it. Oops! The mailbox post split in two, and down it went.

I instantly put the cart in reverse. But when I put it in drive, the cart would not go forward. "Oh no! Your parents are going to flip out. We are stuck in the street, and the golf cart will not go anywhere but backward!" Alex ran from the road to his house to tell his parents, and out they came. My heart skipped a beat. I couldn't imagine the words that were about to be spoken.

"Oh, it's just a mailbox. Let's go in the house and call your mom," Alex's mother said to me.

Then I really became anxious. *Oh dear. Mom is going to be mad when she hears what I did this time on that golf cart,* I thought.

Her reaction when I told her was, "Oh no, not another accident!" After calling my mom, the family asked me to have dinner with them. I was shocked at the offer! After all, I did just hit their mailbox.

Years passed, and I was in the neighborhood on my tricycle. I noticed the "footprint" I left. Their mailbox post stood shorter than all the rest of the mailboxes! *How embarrassing!* I thought. I wondered what they would think if I knocked on the door to not just say "Hi" but once again apologize for my reckless driving ... in my golf cart. Perhaps one day I will have the courage!

# Driver's Training by the Golf Cart

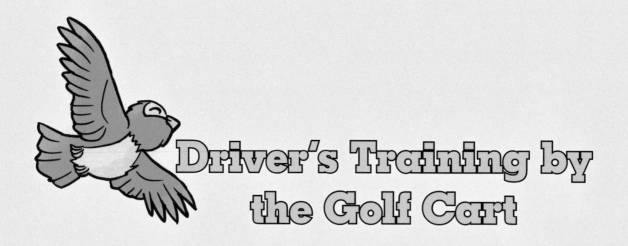

When I bought my golf cart, it was instead of getting a go-kart. Where I lived, go-karts were illegal to drive on streets and sidewalks, while electric golf carts were not. Driving a golf cart at Aunt Sally's gave me the idea of getting one of my own, but Mom thought it was also a way for me to start early for driver's training.

I was thirteen years old when I got my golf cart. Through trial and error, I learned the basics of driving without going the speed of an actual automobile. When I turned age sixteen I signed up for driver's training. Then it was time for everyone around me to really watch out.

I was going from a golf cart that went only about 7 mph at max to at least 70 mph at full speed. That's a significant difference, right? I assured my driver's training instructor there was no need to worry as I had driven my golf cart for a few years. He didn't know what to say and still appeared unsure of me getting behind the wheel of an actual car. Well, unfortunately for him, it became my turn to drive, and behind the wheel I was.

The driving instructor looked like someone strapped in on a huge roller-coaster ride, getting ready for takeoff. He placed both hands flat on the dashboard. I told him to just relax and that I had it all under control. As I began driving, he seemed to get less tense. The next day, he told the other instructors how well I did. I reminded each of them it was because of my golf cart that I knew how to drive. I left out all the accidents I had during my years of driving it!

While these stories are all true, I was lucky to have never gotten hurt. It is always smart to think of safety first. Whether you are riding a bicycle or a driving a golf cart, always let a grown-up know where you are. And wear the proper safety gear, such as a helmet. On the golf cart, I had a sign under the seat in back to let drivers in cars know I was allowed on the road, but the cart didn't move as quickly as they did in their cars! Another safety measure I used while driving my golf cart was to never drive in the dark, which is also an important thing to remember when riding a bicycle. Bicycles and golf carts do not have the safety features as cars or trucks do, such as covered roofs or closed doors and windows to protect you from strange critters that wander around at night. Lastly, during the day, have a friend with you, or at least your pet, like I did. Life is much more fun when you're not alone!

Printed in the United States
By Bookmasters